WISCONSIN

Past and Present

Bridget Heos

rosen publishing's
rosen central®

New York

For Rosie, Aggie, Joe Joe, Jack, and my godson R. J.
And for my cousin Eli, a star quarterback and Packers fan

Published in 2010 by The Rosen Publishing Group, Inc.
29 East 21st Street, New York, NY 10010

Library of Congress Cataloging-in-Publication Data

Heos, Bridget.
Wisconsin: past and present / Bridget Heos.—1st ed.
   p. cm.—(The United States: past and present)
Includes bibliographical references and index.
ISBN-13: 978-1-4358-5293-8 (library binding)
ISBN-13: 978-1-4358-5584-7 (pbk)
ISBN-13: 978-1-4358-5585-4 (6 pack)
1. Wisconsin—Juvenile literature. 2. Wisconsin—History—Juvenile literature.
I. Title.
F581.3.H46 2009
977.5—dc22

2009003906

Manufactured in the United States of America

On the cover: Top left: Wisconsin's largest city, Milwaukee, began as a fur trading post. Top right: Lambeau Field is the home of Wisconsin's football franchise, the Green Bay Packers. Bottom: Dairy farming is a major business in Wisconsin, where, statewide, farmers own 1.23 million head of cattle.

Contents

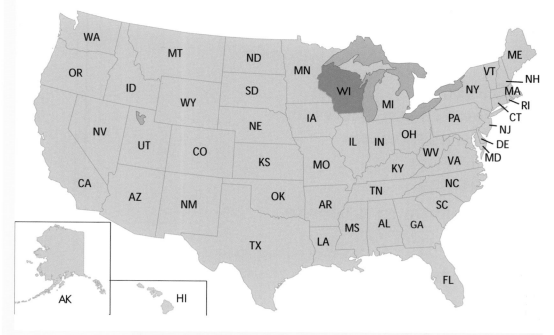

Glacial lakes dot Wisconsin's landscape *(top)*. Wisconsin is bordered by Minnesota, Iowa, Illinois, Lake Michigan, Michigan's Upper Peninsula, and Lake Superior *(bottom)*.

Introduction

In Wisconsin, kids learn to ice-skate soon after learning how to walk. People ride snowmobiles across frozen lakes. Green Bay Packers fans support their team, snow or shine. People not only adapt to the cold weather, but they also enjoy it—at least until the warm summertime rolls around. For those growing up in this upper Midwestern state, weathering the cold is part of the culture.

So are culinary treasures, such as bratwurst, cheddar and Swiss cheeses, fish fries, and supper clubs. Immigrants from European countries like Germany, Poland, Ireland, and Italy gave root to these and other state traditions.

The top industries in Wisconsin have also contributed to its unique flavor. Through agriculture, the state got its reputation for picture-perfect barns and silos and black-and-white cows lazily grazing on grassy fields. Manufacturing has made Milwaukee the city that works. And thanks to the natural beauty of Wisconsin's forests, rivers, and lakes, tourism is the third major moneymaker in the state.

However, before people made their mark on Wisconsin, ice did. From fertile fields to glacial lakes, the last ice age sculpted the state's landscape into what you see today.

Chapter 1

THE GEOGRAPHY OF WISCONSIN

If you ever go to a Green Bay Packers home game, look at the ground beneath you. On the same spot long ago, you would have been standing on ice up to a mile (1.6 kilometers) deep—the equivalent of twelve long city blocks stacked on top of each other.

That's because many times in the past 1.8 million years, and as recently as about fifteen thousand years ago, thick glaciers rolled across Wisconsin, overtaking the land like a slow-moving tsunami. These glaciers, which formed and grew during the ice ages of the Pleistocene epoch, carved Wisconsin's landscape.

The impact the glaciers had on the state is so great that, today, you can hike along a 1,000-mile (1,609 km) Ice Age Trail—all within Wisconsin. Also, almost the entire state is part of the Ice Age National Scientific Reserve.

Glaciers affect the land in two ways. First, they're not made of pure ice, such as the cubes you put in your lemonade. Instead, they contain sand, pebbles, and even boulders. As the glaciers move, this sediment scrapes the land and erodes it, particularly if it's made of soft rock.

The second way that glaciers change the land is by melting and depositing rock and soil. In the Midwest, including parts of Wisconsin, this till (as it is called) created fertile farmland.

Located near Kettle Moraine State Forest in Wisconsin, these drumlins were formed by glacial drifts. Drumlins are one of many landforms in the state caused by glaciation.

Some of the geographical features in Wisconsin that were molded by ice include:

- **Drumlins** Scientists don't know exactly how glaciers caused these elongated hills. However, they run parallel to the way the glacier flowed. In Wisconsin, they can be seen mostly in the southeast of the state. For instance, the state capital, Madison, sits atop a drumlin.
- **Moraines** When the glaciers deposited sand, pebbles, and rock, the sediment formed ridges or hills, also called moraines.

Where is Wisconsin?

The boundaries of Wisconsin are Lake Michigan to the east, the Mississippi River to the west, and, to the south, a line dividing Wisconsin and Illinois. To the northwest, Wisconsin's boundary is in Lake Superior. The Upper Peninsula of Lake Superior, however, belongs to Michigan.

These can be anywhere from 30 to 300 feet (9 to 91 meters) tall. In the north, the moraines form rolling hills, marshes, bogs, and lakes. Perhaps the best known of these landforms is the Kettle Moraine in eastern Wisconsin. It's actually several moraines that formed between the Lake Michigan and Green Bay glacial lobes, which are bodies of ice.

- **Kettles** As the glaciers melted, chunks of ice broke off and got buried in the sand and rock. When these ice blocks melted, they formed lakes called kettles. "Kettle" is the name of an old-fashioned pot.

- **Bay and Peninsula** The Green Bay glacial lobe eroded the soft rock in what is now Green Bay. The area became lowland. When Lake Michigan filled with water, the lowland turned into a bay divided from the rest of the lake by the Door Peninsula. The peninsula did not erode because it's made of harder rock. It is part of the Niagara Escarpment, a ridge that curves through Lakes Michigan and Huron and into Ontario, Canada.

- Lake Michigan was not a lake but low-land during the last ice age. As the glacier filling its basin retreated and melted, moraines formed to the south. Water pooled behind these moraines, becoming the first version of Lake Michigan.
- Lake Superior's basin was created millions of years ago by a large rift within the continent of North America. Glaciers molded the basin, however, and today, Lake Superior is the largest freshwater lake in the world.

A family hikes along the Ice Age Trail, a 1,000-mile (1,609 km) path located entirely within Wisconsin.

The most recent ice age reached its peak just about fifteen thousand years ago and is actually named after the state. During the Wisconsin Glaciation, six glacial lobes gripped the state like icy fingers. They moved at different speeds and reached various points to the south. The Green Bay lobe extended the farthest of all the lobes,

Wisconsin Weather

During the ice age . . .

As the glacier flowed south over Wisconsin, its edge was an icy cliff that was sometimes hundreds of feet high. Freezing winds howled across the glacier, and in the winter, snow fell almost constantly.

In the summer, winds from the Gulf of Mexico collided with cold glacial air, causing torrential downpours. Melting ice cascaded down, creating mudslides. While conditions at the edge of the glacier were extreme, the temperature during this time of year was mild. In fact, if it weren't for the dangerous mudslides (and assuming there wasn't a monsoon), you could have stood beside the glacier and felt fairly comfortable, even though a chilly wind would have whipped against you.

Now . . .

In the winter, Wisconsin still gets snow but not constantly. The greatest snowfall occurs to the north, in the Iron County Snowbelt, which averages 150 to 165 inches (381 to 419 centimeters) a year. That's a lot of snow, but not compared to the mile-deep (1.6 km) glacier covering Wisconsin during the last ice age!

Today, summers in Wisconsin vary in temperature just like the winter snowfall. In the south, the state gets almost twenty days of 90-plus degrees Fahrenheit (32-plus degrees Celsius) weather annually. To the north, the state gets fewer, if any, hot days.

stretching all the way to Janesville in southern Wisconsin. This is because it moved along the lowlands bordering what is now Lake Michigan.

Other lobes stopped before they reached the southwestern two-thirds of the state. This land is called the "Driftless Area," meaning glaciers didn't drift here.

These rocks and boulders were deposited when the glacier from the last ice age melted thousands of years ago. Glaciers carry sediment and rocks that scrape against the terrain, eroding it.

Hold the Ice, Please

Just as water flows downhill, not up, the same is true of glaciers. The southwestern third of Wisconsin was on higher ground than other parts of the state. Therefore, the glacier went around this region.

Glaciers smoothed the rest of Wisconsin—and much of the northern Midwest—like rivers smooth stones. It was also flattened because glacial deposits filled steep valleys. But glaciers didn't touch the Driftless Area. Because of that, its landscape is older and more rugged.

Here, steep valleys and craggy hills cover the land. Dramatic landforms are seen, including a natural sandstone bridge carved by wind, one of the oldest of its kind in the world. And while glacial lakes don't exist here as they do in the rest of the state, several rivers run through the area, including the Wisconsin, Mississippi, and Kickapoo.

About fifteen thousand years ago, the glacier that had overtaken Wisconsin retreated to the north. This doesn't mean it flowed backward into Canada. Rather, the ice melted faster than it could flow southward. It re-advanced ten thousand years ago. But overall, the Wisconsin Glaciation—and, in fact, the entire Pleistocene epoch—was ending.

By about 12,500 years ago, people had followed the edge of the retreating glacier into Wisconsin. These first peoples, called Paleo-Indians, lived in the region for five thousand years and marked a new era for Wisconsin: a human era.

Since the ice melted, people like the Paleo-Indians have found a land abundant with food and natural resources, whether in the northern forests and central plains, or on the coasts of lakes Michigan and Superior, or the Driftless Area to the southwest. In the following chapters, you'll learn how hunting, fur trapping, mining, logging, dairy farming, brewing, manufacturing, and outdoor recreation all played important roles in the human history of Wisconsin.

Chapter 2

THE HISTORY OF WISCONSIN

For thousands of years, the first Wisconsinites—the Paleo-Indians—survived a changing climate, dangerous hunts, and the disappearance of animals that they depended on for food. Their spear points, found in the state, date back to around 12,500 years ago.

Through the years, they spread out into different regions and developed unique cultures. In Wisconsin, many descendants of Paleo-Indians hunted in the winter and fished during the summer. Though nomads, they returned to the same places each season to hunt and gather. Semipermanent villages arose.

One prominent group during this time was the Effigy Mounds people. They're named for their mounds, which are shaped as animals or arranged like the solar system. Some archaeologists think these were burial sites; others think they marked territory.

Whatever the case, the people revolutionized their lifestyle when they began growing crops like corn and using the bow and arrow. This allowed them to hunt and harvest more efficiently.

As food became more plentiful, people stayed in one place and grew in numbers. As time went on, roots grew deeper. Every act of settling down seemingly led to another. With more people to feed, they cooperated to harvest more crops. Because they had enough food, the people stayed and built more permanent homes. To protect

When Middle Mississippians moved to Wisconsin, they met the Woodland people. The two groups shared a village in Aztalan.

those homes, they battled other groups for territory.

Though it seemed like these acts would make the Effigy Mounds people a permanent fixture in Wisconsin, it didn't. Their culture eventually changed, maybe because of contact with people they traded with. They became the Woodland people; some settled in a place called Aztalan.

The area was actually home to two groups. People called the Middle Mississippians had been living in a large city—bigger than Paris or Rome at the time—around present-day St. Louis. They moved north around 1000 CE, settling parts of Illinois and Wisconsin. One place they settled was Aztalan, the village already occupied by the Woodland people. Whether peacefully or through war, the two groups came to live together in the village. The 20-acre (8.09 hectares) village site can be seen today in the Aztalan State Park.

About two hundred years after it was settled, the city was mysteriously abandoned. A new people, the Oneota, soon spread out across the Midwest. Some archaeologists think this group was a merger of the Middle Mississippians and the Woodland people. These archaeologists also think the Oneota could be ancestors of the modern Ioway and Ho-chunk tribes, the latter being one of the tribes living in Wisconsin today.

Everything Changes

After Christopher Columbus' voyage to the Americas, the Spanish took over the Caribbean and Gulf Coast. Soon, the English settled in New England and along the Atlantic Coast. So when the French took to the sea to get a piece of the "New World," they headed north to what would become Canada. They named their territory New France.

Jean Nicolet was apparently the first Frenchman to arrive in Wisconsin in 1634. Landing in Green Bay, he would have met a tribe called the Menominee, which lived around the area. He had been sent by Samuel de Champlain, the governor of New France, to find

Jean Nicolet came to Wisconsin from New France and came upon the Menominee tribe. The arrival of Europeans destroyed the tribal way of life.

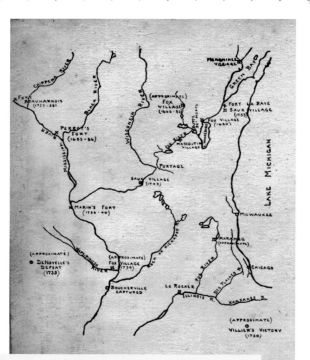

This map marks the locations of the Fox Indian Wars. Because of competition for fur and land, war was common in early Wisconsin.

the Pacific Ocean and Asia. Needless to say, he didn't find it. He did find fur, which the French planned to export to Montreal, and from there, to France. But soon, they also found themselves in the middle of a war.

The Iroquois Indians were attacking the French and tribes to the north in pursuit of fur, which they would then trade with the Dutch. The war spilled over into Wisconsin. Transporting fur from Wisconsin to Montreal was too dangerous. The fur trade would have to wait.

After about twenty years, with the war subsiding, fur trading became a thriving industry. At the time, demand for fur was great. It wasn't to make lavish fur coats but rather simple felt hats that Europeans and others could wear to work in the fields. Beaver pelts were the most sought-after furs, and they were, at the time, plentiful in Wisconsin.

Trading posts were established along the Mississippi and Great Lakes, including in Green Bay. There, Europeans imported goods like cooking tools, guns, and blankets, which they traded with Native

Green Bay

In the early 1800s . . .

Green Bay looked like a cluster of farms. Homes lined the Fox River, on which fur was shipped to Montreal. French, Métis, and Native Americans still lived there in relative peace, even though, for the latter, the fur trade had taken its toll on the traditional way of life.

Green Bay changed after America won the War of 1812. At that point, settlers from the eastern states (Yankees) and Europeans arrived more steadily. Soon, Native American tribes were pushed off their land. Meanwhile, settlement continued, with the population growing to 1,644 by 1855.

Now . . .

The Fox River divides Green Bay into east and west sides, connected by four bridges. While the water no longer is used to transport fur, it is a draw for many weekend fishermen and boaters. The population of Green Bay has grown to a little more than 100,000. It is the smallest town in America to have a professional football team.

The population of Green Bay grew in 1867 to at least 1,600 due to the arrival of Europeans and Yankees.

American hunters for fur. Tribes became dependent on these things, and their lives changed. To find fur, they traveled far afield from the land they had been farming and hunting. This broke up families and communities. Women and children relocated to trading post towns, where they were exploited and exposed to diseases. Tribes battled for food and fur, and they formed alliances with the French or British, who battled each other for control of New France. Because of war and disease, tribal populations dwindled.

At the same time, there was a mingling of cultures. Native Americans and the French married. In most fur-trading towns around the Great Lakes, mixed-race (or Métis) people were the majority. For instance, 60 percent of the Green Bay population in 1824 was Métis. Some ran the fur trade, becoming wealthy businesspeople. On the lower socioeconomic end, others transported furs. Together, they created a unique culture that blended French and Indian language, customs, and beliefs.

In 1763, Britain wrested control of New France and the Wisconsin region from the French. By that time, many Indian Nations had been devastated by colonization. Pontiac, an Ottawa chief, united tribes from Kentucky to Wisconsin and tried to drive British governments back to the Atlantic Ocean, but the war stalled in Detroit and failed.

The fur trade continued, with the French still active participants. Finally, overhunting led to its decline around 1840. New industries, equally strong, would develop in Wisconsin, which you'll read about in chapter 4. The region would begin its journey toward statehood, which you'll learn about next. The Wisconsin tribes who had adapted for thousands of years to life on the northern frontier, however, would never be the same.

Chapter 3

THE GOVERNMENT OF WISCONSIN

Wisconsin was the thirtieth state to enter the Union. It happened in 1848—eleven years after Michigan to the east and ten years before Minnesota to the west. Today, Michigan is led by a governor, a thirty-three-member state senate, and a ninety-nine-member state assembly. The governor has the most powerful line-item veto authority in the country. When he gets a bill from the state legislature, he doesn't have to accept or reject it as a whole. Instead, he can change the bill by crossing out lines or words.

The people are represented in the federal government by two senators and eight representatives. Once a Republican stronghold, the state now leans somewhat to the left. It voted for the Democratic presidential candidate in the last six elections, and Democrats make up the majority of Wisconsin's U.S. senators and representatives. It has elected mostly Democratic governors since the 1950s. However, the political makeup of the state legislature has varied, and it's considered a swing state.

The two parties don't tell the whole story of Wisconsin politics. Regionally and nationally, the state has been a leader in third political parties. Even within the predominate parties, Wisconsin leaders have pursued innovative programs. Here are some examples of groundbreaking politics in Wisconsin:

This 1854 poster united those against "having the free soil of Wisconsin become a hunting ground for human kidnappers."

The Birth of the Republican Party In 1854, members of various political groups met in Ripon, Wisconsin, to protest the Kansas-Nebraska Bill. If passed, it would allow slavery in the two territories. The majority of Wisconsin residents objected to this. The bill also would have prevented non-citizens in the territory from voting. Many Wisconsinites were recent immigrants and opposed this, too. At the meeting in Ripon, leaders agreed to form a new party. Later that year, a convention was held in Madison to organize the newly named Republican Party. Almost immediately, the party became the majority in the state assembly. The next year, a Republican governor was elected.

A Progressive Stronghold In the early 1900s, Governor Robert "Fighting Bob" La Follette led the Progressive Party. An offshoot of the Republican Party, it demanded decisions to be made based on reason and evidence, rather than on favors being exchanged. It also promoted an efficient government. Later led by La Follette's sons, the party lasted in Wisconsin until 1946, when most members became Democrats. Today, La Follette and his wife, Belle, would be called a "power couple."

After having their first child, Belle went to law school and became her husband's advisor. She was also a leader in the women's movement. Robert La Follette appointed several women to state offices, which was one of the movement's goals.

Women's Rights Leader Wisconsin congressmen supported women's right to vote, and when the Nineteenth Amendment was passed in 1919, Wisconsin was the first state to ratify it.

Robert M. La Follette Sr., seen here campaigning in Cumberland, Wisconsin, in 1897, led the state's powerful Progressive Party.

The First Socialist City In May 1886, workers across the nation agitated for an eight-hour workday. During the protest at a steel foundry in Milwaukee, five protestors were killed and four wounded by state troops. Soon after, workers formed the People's Party. In 1897, it merged with the city's Socialist Party, which wanted the government to take over industry. But in the meantime, it wanted cleaner and safer conditions for workers and urban dwellers. When the city elected a Socialist mayor and other Socialist candidates in 1910, it became America's first Socialist city. Nineteen forty was the last year the city had a Socialist mayor, but for decades, the party influenced Milwaukee politics.

A Conservative Think Tank Tommy Thompson, a Republican who became governor in 1986, started programs that later would be instated across the country. These included Wisconsin Works,

Victor Berger (*right*) led the Socialist Party in Milwaukee. In 1910, the city elected a Socialist mayor and many other Socialist candidates.

which was a forerunner to national welfare reform, and Wisconsin's Council on Model Academic Standards, which was similar to the future No Child Left Behind Act.

Birthplace of Earth Day In 1962, Wisconsin's U.S. Senator Gaylord Nelson proposed an amendment granting Americans the right to a good environment. In response, the U.S. Congress established the Environmental Protection (EPA) Agency and passed the Water Quality Improvement Act and the Air Quality Control Act. In 1969, Nelson went on to encourage people to spend a day teaching and learning about the environment. Earth Day was born.

The Road to Statehood

Before its government leaders could be innovators, Wisconsin had to become a state. Here's how it happened:

When we left off in chapter 2, the British had wrested control of what is now Wisconsin from the French. Many French traders remained in Wisconsin. The majority of the population, however, was Native American or Métis. Most Wisconsinites focused on maintaining their livelihood through the fur trade. When the Revolutionary

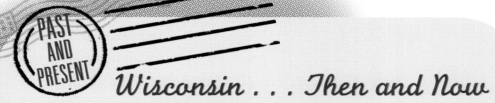

PAST AND PRESENT

Wisconsin . . . Then and Now

At the time of statehood . . .

In 1848, Wisconsin became a state, with a population of just 155,277. Top industries included farming, logging, and mining. The University of Wisconsin was founded the same year. Soon after, the first graduating class had just two students. While about a third of Wisconsinites were foreign born, they came from only ten countries. Germans, Irish, and Norwegians were major ethnic groups.

Now . . .

Today, Wisconsin has approximately 5.4 million residents, and about forty-two thousand students attend the University of Wisconsin-Madison. Farming is still a top industry, but logging and mining have been replaced by manufacturing and tourism. While many nationalities are now represented in Wisconsin, German roots are still strong, with about 50 percent of residents claiming German heritage—more than anyplace else in the country.

War was won and America achieved independence, none of this changed much.

Then, in 1787, the thirteen colonies adopted the Northwest Ordinance. While it didn't affect Wisconsin right away, it would later. At the time, Wisconsin was not a colony but part of America's Northwest Territory. The ordinance made rules for how territories should establish governments. It said that if a territory had more than sixty thousand inhabitants, it could become a state.

The ordinance also described how land should be sold to settlers. From 1832 to 1866, the land was divided for sale. That's when things

James Doty lobbied state legislators to choose Madison as the state capital. The Capitol building is shown here.

really started to change. While newcomers settled onto Wisconsin land, government treaties pushed Native Americans off their lands.

As Wisconsin's population increased, it became its own territory, rather than sharing with areas like Michigan. Henry Dodge was appointed the first governor of the territory in 1836. The race was on to choose a capital city. James Doty, a politician and land surveyor originally from New York, won the bid and Madison became the capital.

From 1836 to 1846, Wisconsin's population grew from 11,683 to 155,277. Now, Wisconsin could become a state. But first, the territory had to establish a state constitution. After much arguing, the first draft, which gave property rights to women and laid the foundation for future black voting rights, was completed. It didn't pass. The second draft, which omitted both items, was considered less radical and passed in 1848. Wisconsin was a state.

As of the last U.S. Census, Wisconsin's population was about 5.4 million, with the two largest cities being Milwaukee and Madison. The state's population explosion led to several new industries, which we'll talk about in the next chapter.

Chapter 4

THE INDUSTRIES OF WISCONSIN

When the Wisconsin fur trade declined in the early 1800s, European and Yankee settlers turned to lead mining. Native Americans had mined southwest Wisconsin for centuries. Now, the metal was needed for construction and ammunition.

Easily accessible lead eventually ran out. Mining continued in the north and, on a smaller scale, in the south, but many miners moved on. Settlers in 1830s and '40s turned to agriculture—first wheat (from 1840 to 1880, Wisconsin was known as "America's Bread Basket"), then cranberries, tobacco, feed crops, fruit and vegetables, and dairy.

Wisconsin is well known today for its dairy farms. That trend started in the 1860s, when insects attacked wheat crops and farmers searched for alternatives. In the meantime, New York farmers had moved to Wisconsin, bringing their dairy know-how with them. German and Scandinavian immigrants were also adept dairy farmers. By 1899, more than 90 percent of Wisconsin farmers raised dairy cattle.

Cheese making began as a way to keep milk from spoiling. The idea caught on, and soon, many towns revolved around a church, school, and cheese factory (where the cheese makers and their families also lived). From there, cheese was shipped to Green Bay and on to England and elsewhere.

Wisconsin cranberry bogs like these produce 60 percent of the nation's supply of the fruit. The cranberry industry contributes $350 million to the state economy.

The state is still a top producer of both dairy and vegetables worldwide. In fact, bringing in $80 billion a year, agriculture is the number-one industry in Wisconsin. Corporate farms have largely replaced family enterprises, but small farms are making a comeback—this time as organic farms.

While agriculture thrived in southern Wisconsin, logging became a major industry in the northern part of the state. Pine trees were floated down the Wisconsin River to mills, which processed them by harnessing water power. Towns grew around these mills. Then, the pine was shipped down the river, where it was used to build schools, houses, churches, and other structures throughout the Midwest. As demand increased, logging practices became more aggressive. Soon, the forests were depleted.

However, the forests gave birth to two thriving industries. One was paper manufacturing, an offshoot of the lumber industry in Wisconsin. Today, the state is the number-one paper producer in the nation, with 12 percent of American paper coming from Wisconsin.

In terms of forests, the North Woods initially struggled after the decline of lumber. The land wasn't good for farming, and towns sunk into economic depressions. Then, the forests grew back. This time, instead of cutting them down, people left them alone. They encouraged tourists to escape workaday city life to fish, hunt, and camp in the wilds of Wisconsin. Today, tourism brings in $12 billion every year.

A major industry in the 1800s, logging declined as the forests in northern Wisconsin became depleted. But papermaking is still a big business.

Milwaukee: The City That Works

In the mid-1800s, many Milwaukee companies processed wheat into flour because that's what Wisconsin farmers were growing. When wheat farms declined, new manufacturing plants took the place of flour processing plants. Soon, Milwaukee workers were building machinery and other supplies for companies throughout the country. So many Milwaukeeans had manufacturing jobs that by 1881, the city referred to itself as "The City That Works."

Milwaukee was also the most foreign city in America. By 1910, three-fourths of its residents were immigrants or the children of immigrants. Germans and Poles were the top two ethnic groups, but other countries were represented. People congregated around others from their home country, and ethnic neighborhoods developed.

Meanwhile, the number of laborers put the city on the cutting edge of worker's rights. It was the first state in the nation to pass an unemployment compensation bill. During the Great Depression, this bill and the Labor Party, combined with the city's Socialist Party, influenced city government for decades.

One industry that Milwaukee has always been known for is beer. For German and other European immigrants arriving in the 1800s, breweries were an important part of the community, just like churches and schools. Breweries held festivals and sponsored athletic teams. By the Civil War, Wisconsin had 160 breweries, and Milwaukee became the beer capital of America.

In 1919, Prohibition, which disallowed the manufacture of alcohol, hurt Wisconsin breweries and taverns. Later, a U.S. senator from Wisconsin proposed an amendment to end Prohibition. It passed, and in 1933, brewers were back in business.

The P. H. Best Brewing Company, shown here in late nineteenth-century Milwaukee, was one of the many breweries to thrive in Wisconsin.

But the country was in the grips of the Great Depression. In Milwaukee, 75 percent of people had lost their jobs. Only during World War II did Wisconsin's industry grow robust again.

In the 1970s and '80s, Milwaukee was struck by more hard times when factories closed or relocated overseas. Showing Wisconsin's knack for adapting to economic downturns, many Milwaukee companies shifted from domestic goods to exports. Today, manufacturing remains one of the state's top industries, bringing in $37.1 billion.

Products have changed through the years, but Wisconsin's pride in its workers remains. In fact, many sports teams are named for

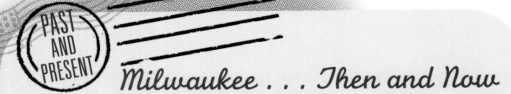

Milwaukee . . . Then and Now

At the turn of the twentieth century . . .

The population of Milwaukee circa 1900 was about 285,000. Germans, the majority, settled on the city's north side. While on the south side, the Polish community grew in 1906 to seventy thousand, becoming the second-largest ethnic group. The neighborhood became known for a house style called the "Polish flat." First, Polish immigrants would build a four-room cottage. Then, after saving more money, they would raise it up and build a basement apartment, which they would rent. Once the house was paid for, the original family would no longer rent the basement. Now, they had a bigger house.

Most immigrants worked in factories. At the same time, some families, such as Pabst and Usinger, became wealthy owners of breweries and other companies.

Now . . .

The population in Milwaukee is about 600,000. Greater Milwaukee, which includes four counties within and surrounding the city, has about 1.5 million residents. While many Milwaukeeans claim German or Polish ancestry, the city is more diverse than ever. African Americans now make up about 16 percent of the population, and Latinos and Asians, representing a new wave of immigrants, have settled in the old Polish neighborhood on the south side.

Manufacturing employs the second-highest number of workers in the city, but many products coming out of Milwaukee are decidedly more high tech than at the turn of the century.

them. The Green Bay Packers got their name from meat packers. The University of Wisconsin Badgers are named for lead miners. And when the Seattle Pilots moved to Wisconsin, they were renamed the Milwaukee Brewers.

Chapter 5

PEOPLE FROM WISCONSIN: PAST AND PRESENT

Many people from Wisconsin have made their mark on history, literature, sports, entertainment, and business. Here are just some of their stories:

Historical Leaders

Black Hawk (1767–1858) Black Hawk was a Sauk chief who took a stand against a treaty that pushed the Sauk and Fox off of their Wisconsin and Illinois lands. Black Hawk believed the treaty, signed in 1804, wasn't valid. When the treaty went into effect in the 1820s, he led a battle to regain tribal lands. The battle ended tragically when American troops ignored the Sauk's white flag of surrender and massacred hundreds of people, including women and children. Overwhelmed by U.S. military force, the Sauk and other tribes were forced to surrender their land.

Solomon Juneau (1793–1856) Solomon Juneau was a French fur trader who, in 1818, founded a trading post in the Native American village that is now Milwaukee. He later purchased land surrounding the post and became its first

31

Black Hawk, a Sauk chief, battled American troops for tribal lands, a stand that ended with the tragic massacre of many Sauk people.

mayor. He is widely regarded as the father of Milwaukee. With his wife, Josette, the granddaughter of a Menomonee chief, Juneau was also the father of thirteen children.

Jacques Marquette (1637–1675) Jacques Marquette, a Jesuit missionary, explored the Mississippi River in 1673 with fur trader Louis Joliet. During their journey, the Arkansas Indians warned Marquette and Joliet that farther south, they'd face gun-toting foreigners. The two travelers realized the Arkansas were referring to the Spanish, who occupied the Gulf of Mexico. They headed back to Quebec with news that the Mississippi led to the sea. Years later, Marquette University in Milwaukee was named for the explorer.

Jean Nicolet (1598–1642) Jean Nicolet is thought to be the first European to have arrived in Wisconsin. Fluent in several Native American languages, he was sent by Champlain in 1634 to promote peace between the Winnebago and Huron tribes and to find the Pacific Ocean. Nicolet was considered to be more interested in church and country than his own self-interests. In 1642, his boat capsized in the St. Lawrence River. Though famous for his sailing expeditions, his last words were, "I can't swim."

Entertainers

Willem Dafoe (1955–) Actor Willem Dafoe, who portrayed the Green Goblin in the movie *Spider-Man*, was born in Appleton, Wisconsin.

Chris Farley (1964–1997) Comedian Chris Farley was born in Madison and attended Marquette University.

Heather Graham (1970–) Actress Heather Graham was born to a strict family in Milwaukee but moved around a lot, as her father was in the Federal Bureau of Investigation (FBI).

Harry Houdini (1874–1926) While born in Budapest, Hungary, magician Harry Houdini grew up

Harry Houdini, shown here in 1912, prepares for one of his greatest feats: escaping handcuffs while in a box under the East River in New York.

in Appleton and Milwaukee, where at age nine he performed his first public show, a trapeze act.

Tony Shalhoub (1953–) Tony Shalhoub, the title character of TV's *Monk*, grew up the second youngest of ten children in Green Bay. Both of his parents were from Lebanon.

Spencer Tracy (1900–1967) Famous leading man Spencer Tracy, a Milwaukee native, attended Marquette University.

Orson Welles (1915–1985) *Citizen Kane* star Orson Welles was born in Kenosha, but at the age of nine, he left with his father to travel the world.

Sports Figures

Brett Favre (1969–) Wisconsin lost one of its perennial sports figures in 2008 when Brett Favre retired and then, upon returning to the National Football League (NFL), was traded to the New York Jets. While born in Mississippi, Favre played for the Green Bay Packers for sixteen years. During his first game, he threw a 35-yard pass with thirteen seconds left, winning the game. The three-time Most Valuable Player (MVP) earned the loyalty of fans, but his retirement and return to the NFL drew mixed reactions.

Vince Lombardi (1913–1970) When Vince Lombardi became head coach of the Green Bay Packers, the team had won just one game the year before. Three years later, Lombardi and quarterback Bart Starr led the Packers to a

Super Bowl victory. Lombardi was known for trying new things on the field. For instance, he once had his players switch jerseys in order to confuse the Chicago Bears. However, his main strategies were inspirational leadership, hard work, and toughness. He said, "It's not whether you get knocked down; it's whether you get up." During his nine years of coaching, the Packers were 98-30-04. After Lombardi died in 1970, the Super Bowl trophy was named in his honor.

Writers and Artists

Lizzie Black Kander (1858–1940) Lizzie Black Kander, a Jewish American Milwaukeean, was president of the Settlement, a program that taught Jewish immigrants about the American way of life. To raise money for the organization, she published *The Settlement Cookbook: The Way to a Man's Heart*. It went on to sell 1.5 million copies and was a staple in American households.

The author Laura Ingalls Wilder, shown here, set her first book, *Little House in the Big Woods*, in her birth state of Wisconsin.

The Green Bay Packers

In 1919 . . .

When a meat packer named Curly Lambeau placed an ad in the paper seeking football players, twenty-five rough-and-tumble guys showed up. They were the first Green Bay Packers. Only in those days, they were called the Green Bay Indians, after the company that sponsored the uniforms. Acme Packing bought out Indian Packing, and the team became the Packers.

Because they were killing all the local teams, the Packers joined the NFL. In those days, lots of small towns had teams in the league. But eventually, only Green Bay remained, thanks to community support and the go-getter attitude of Lambeau.

People dressed up for the games. Ladies wore dresses, high heels, and fur coats, and men wore suits. At half time, they showed off their outfits by promenading around the field.

Now . . .

People no longer parade around the field at halftime. Instead, the big social event at Lambeau Field is tailgating before the game. Fans wear jerseys and "cheese head" hats. Players are chosen through a draft pick. However, the people of Green Bay still support their team. The Packers are the only community-owned team in the NFL.

When opposing teams' fans called Wisconsinites "cheese heads," one man started a "cheese head" company. Today, many fans wear the hats.

Laura Ingalls Wilder (1867–1957) Laura Ingalls Wilder was born in Pepin, Wisconsin, which is the setting of her first book, *Little House in the Big Woods*. Her daughter Rose, an author, encouraged Wilder to write the book, which was published when she was sixty-five years old. Since then, the Little House series has been translated into forty languages.

Frank Lloyd Wright (1867–1959) Architect Frank Lloyd Wright grew up in Richland Center and Madison, and spent time on a family farm in Spring Green. An architect, he believed that America should have a distinct style of architecture, rather than copying Europe. His style employed natural elements, such as stone, and followed natural forms, such as the flatness of prairies. After living in Chicago, Wright returned to Spring Green to open an architecture school.

Business People

William Harley (1880–1943) and Arthur Davidson (1881–1950) William Harley and Arthur Davidson built the first Harley-Davidson motorcycle in a small wooden shed in

This 1899 poster advertises the "funny, wonderful elephant brass band" of the Ringling Bros. Circus.

1903. By 1907, two of Davidson's brothers, Walter and William, had joined the Milwaukee company, which now employed eighteen workers. Soon, motorcycle buyers included racers, policemen, and soldiers. The company grew, and its headquarters are still in Milwaukee.

The Ringling Brothers of Baraboo, Wisconsin, held their first circus in their backyard. Soon, the seven brothers, Al, Alf, Charles, John, Otto, Henry, and Gus, were running one of the largest traveling circuses in America. The full name of the show was (take a deep breath) "Ringling Bros. United Monster Shows, Great Double Circus, Royal European Menagerie, Museum, Caravan, and Congress of Trained Animals." It eventually merged with the Barnum & Bailey Circus and became known simply as "the Greatest Show on Earth."

Wisconsinites

While many Wisconsinites have become famous, what gives the state its unique flavor is the ordinary people and the things they do. When their work is done, people enjoy bowling leagues, ice skating, Friday night fish fries, fishing and hunting, and professional football, basketball, and baseball. Wisconsin is a state that works hard and plays hard together. Its people have formed strong communities. And historically, when times were tough, they pushed forward together. Perhaps that is why the state motto is just one word: "Forward."

Timeline

1000 CE Middle Mississippians to the south come to Wisconsin and settle in Aztalan.

800 CE Woodland people, possibly a combination of Middle Mississippians and northern tribes, begin living in Wisconsin.

1634 Jean Nicolet, a Frenchman, arrives in Green Bay, probably as the first European explorer.

1650s French fur trapping and trading begin in Wisconsin.

1763 The British wrest control of northern territory, including Wisconsin, from France.

1830s and 1940s Wheat becomes a major crop; in Milwaukee, processing wheat is a major industry.

1840s Due to overhunting, the fur trade moves on to other states.

1848 Wisconsin becomes a state.

1856 The Republican Party forms during a convention in Wisconsin.

1860s As wheat crops fail, vegetable growing and dairy farming take hold.

Late 1800s In northern Wisconsin, logging is a major industry.

1886 The Bay View Massacre occurs.

1897 In Milwaukee, the Labor Party merges with the Socialist Party, which eventually runs the city.

1919 Prohibition cripples the numerous breweries in Wisconsin; the Green Bay Packers are founded.

1929–1930s The Great Depression causes a 75 percent job loss in Milwaukee.

1970 The Seattle Pilots move to Milwaukee and are renamed the Brewers.

1970s and '80s Due to closing and moving factories, manufacturing suffers in Milwaukee; companies eventually focus on exports and thrive once more.

1986 Republican Tommy Thompson becomes governor.

2000 Census shows Wisconsin population to be 5,363,675.

2006 Democratic governor Jim Doyle is reelected with more votes than any other candidate for governor in Wisconsin history.

State motto	"Forward."
State capital	Madison
State flower	The wood violet
State bird	The robin
Statehood date and number	1848, thirtieth
State nickname	"The Badger State"
Total area and U.S. rank	With 54,375 square miles (140,830 sq km), it is the twenty-sixth largest state.
Approximate population at most recent U.S. Census	5,363,675
Length of coastline	575 miles (925 km) of mainland (820 miles/1,319 km including islands)
Highest elevation	Timms Hill, at 1,952 feet (594 m)
Lowest elevation	The shore of Lake Michigan, at 581 feet (177 m)
Major rivers	Mississippi River, Wisconsin River, Fox River

State Flag

State Seal

Major lakes	Lake Superior, Lake Michigan, Lake Winnebago
Hottest temperature recorded	114°F (45°C), at Wisconsin Dells, 1936
Coldest temperature recorded	–55°F (12°C), at Couderay, 1996
Origin of state name	French explorers heard "Wisconsin" used in conversation by a native tribe. It probably meant "river of red stone."
Chief agricultural products	Dairy, vegetables
Major industries	Manufacturing, agriculture, tourism

State Bird

State Flower

GLOSSARY

badger A burrowing animal and the nickname given to lead miners (and the state of Wisconsin) because they apparently mined and lived in hillside burrows.

Democrat One of the two major political parties in America. In general, Democrats believe in more government involvement.

Earth Day A day set aside to learn about environmental issues. Former Wisconsin senator Gaylord Nelson recommended that America have such a day.

glacier A large sheet of ice or snow that develops and spreads when snowfall exceeds the rate of melting.

ice age Any of the time periods during which glaciers covered a large part of the earth.

labor Wage-earning workers; when capitalized, a political party that supports the rights of workers.

line-item veto The power vested in a governor to cross out words or lines in pending litigation.

manufacturing The making of something, usually with machines.

moraines Hills or ridges formed when silt was deposited by melting glaciers.

packers Workers who processed meat; the name of the Green Bay football team.

Progressive A political party that believed in efficient, ethical governing.

Republican One of the two major political parties in America. In general, Republicans believe in less government involvement.

Socialist The political party that believes in government ownership of businesses and services.

state A region in America that is part of the United States, but in some matters, governs itself.

state constitution The laws by which a state governs itself.

territory In the United States, a region of the country that has its own legislature but not the full benefits of states.

Wisconsin Glaciation The last ice age. It was named after the state because its effects are seen more in Wisconsin than anywhere else.

women's suffrage Women's right to vote.

Ice Age Park and Trail Foundation

2110 Main Street

Cross Plains, WI 53528

(800) 227-0046

Web site: http://www.iceagetrail.org

This foundation protects the Ice Age Trail and provides information about hiking on it.

Milwaukee Public Museum

800 West Wells Street

Milwaukee, WI 53233

(800) 700-9069

Web site: http://www.mpm.edu

This museum features nationally and regionally themed exhibits.

Wisconsin Dairy Producers

8418 Excelsior Drive

Madison, WI 53717

(608) 836-8820

Web site: http://www.wisdairy.com

This industry group supplies information about dairy products.

Web Sites

Due to the changing nature of Internet links, Rosen Publishing has developed an online list of Web sites related to the subject of this book. This site is updated regularly. Please use this link to access the list:

http://www.rosenlinks.com/uspp/wipp

FOR FURTHER READING

Apps, Jerry. *Tents, Tigers, and the Ringling Brothers*. Madison, WI: Wisconsin Historical Society, 2006.

Barnes, Pete. *Harley and the Davidsons: Motorcycle Legends*. Madison, WI: Wisconsin Historical Society, 2007.

Bratvold, Gretchen. *Wisconsin*. New York, NY: Lerner, 2001.

Holliday, Diane. *Mountain Wolf Woman: A Ho-Chunk Girlhood*. Madison, WI: Wisconsin Historical Society, 2007.

Kann, Bob. *Lizzie Kander and Her Cookbook*. Madison, WI: Wisconsin Historical Society, 2006.

Koestler-Grack, Rachel. *Brett Favre*. New York, NY: Checkmark Books, 2008.

Ling, Bettina. *Wisconsin*. New York, NY: Children's Press, 2008.

Loew, Patty. *Indian Nations of Wisconsin: Histories of Endurance and Renewal*. Madison, WI: Wisconsin Historical Society, 2001.

Stotts, Stuart. *Curly Lambeau: Building the Green Bay Packers*. Madison, WI: Wisconsin Historical Society, 2007.

Wilder, Laura Ingalls. *Little House Nine-Book Box Set*. New York, NY: HarperTrophy, 2007.

BIBLIOGRAPHY

Choose Milwaukee. "Seven County Region Population and Demographics." Retrieved November 5, 2008 (http://www.choosemilwaukee.com/population.aspx).

Discover Milwaukee. "The Area's Roots." Retrieved November 3, 2008 (http://www.discovermilwaukee.com/living/arearoots.asp).

Dutch, Steven "The Niagara Escarpment." University of Wisconsin-Green Bay. Retrieved September 3, 2008 (http://www.uwgb.edu/DutchS/GEOLWISC/niagesc.htm).

Fleming, Anthony. "Freeze Frame: The Ice Age in Indiana." Indiana Geological Survey. Retrieved September 3, 2008 (http://igs.indiana.edu/Geology/ancient/freezeframe/index.cfm).

Frank Lloyd Wright Foundation. "Biography." Retrieved November 17, 2008 (http://www.cmgww.com/historic/flw/bio.html).

Fritz, Angela. "Lizzie Black Kander & Culinary Reform in Milwaukee." *Wisconsin Magazine of History*, Spring 2004. Retrieved November 17, 2008 (http://www.wisconsinhistory.org/wmh/pdf/spring04_fritz.pdf).

Harley-Davidson. "Timeline." Retrieved November 17, 2008 (http://www.harley-davidson.com/wcm/Content/Pages/H-D_History/history_2000s.jsp?locale=en_US).

Ice Age Park & Trail Foundation. "Home Page." Retrieved September 1, 2008 (http://www.iceagetrail.org).

Jasperse, Patrick. "Line-Item Veto Appears Headed for Approval." *Milwaukee Journal*, March 23, 1995. Retrieved November 2, 2008 (http://findarticles.com/p/articles/mi_qn4207/is_19950323/ai_n10190121).

Jung, Patrick. "French Indian Intermarriage and the Creation of Métis Society." Marquette University. Retrieved September 8, 2008 (http://www.uwgb.edu/wisfrench/library/articles/metis.htm).

Kenny, Judith. "Picturing Milwaukee's Neighborhoods." Collections at University of Wisconsin-Milwaukee Library. Retrieved November 4, 2008 (http://www.uwm.edu/Library/digilib/Milwaukee/records/picture.html).

Laura Ingalls Wilder Memorial Society. "Frequently Asked Questions." Retrieved November 17, 2008 (http://www.liwms.com).

Metropolitan Milwaukee Association of Commerce. "Milwaukee Metro Facts." Retrieved November 19, 2008 (http://www.mmac.org/ImageLibrary/User/bmayborne/Metro_facts_05i_pdf.pdf).

Michigan.gov. "Shorelines of the Great Lakes." Retrieved November 10, 2008 (http://www.michigan.gov/deq/0,1607,7-135-3313_3677-15959--,00.html).

Milwaukee Public Museum. "Indian Country Wisconsin: You Are Here." Retrieved November 3, 2008 (http://www.mpm.edu/wirp).

National Park Service. "Wisconsin's Glacial Legacy." Retrieved September 3, 2008 (http://www.nps.gov/archive/iatr/expanded/history.htm).

PBS. "People and Events: Jacques Marquette (1637–1675) and Louis Joliet (1646–1700)." *American Experience: Chicago: City of the Century*. Retrieved November 16, 2008 (http://www.pbs.org/wgbh/amex/chicago/peopleevents/p_mandj.html).

Red Orbit. "Green Bay Packers Quarterback Brett Favre Retires After 17 Seasons." March 4, 2008. Retrieved November 17, 2008 (http://www.redorbit.com/news/sports/1281244/green_bay_packers_qb_brett_favre_retires_after_17_seasons/index.html).

Rodesch, Jerrold. "Jean Nicolet." *Voyager*, Spring 1984. Retrieved November 15, 2008 (http://www.uwgb.edu/wisfrench/library/articles/nicolet.htm).

The Smithsonian. "Spotlight: Biography, American Indians." Retrieved November 15, 2008 (http://www.smithsonianeducation.org/spotlight/nativeam.html).

Theresa Historical Society. "Solomon Juneau: Founder of Milwaukee." Retrieved November 15, 2008 (http://www.uwgb.edu/wisfrench/library/history/juneau/index.htm).

Thompson, Todd. "After the Thaw: The Development of Lake Michigan." Indiana Geological Survey. Retrieved September 1, 2008 (http://igs.indiana.edu/geology/ancient/afterthaw/index.cfm).

U.S. Environmental Protection Agency. "The Ice Age [Pleistocene Epoch]." Retrieved September 3, 2008 (http://www.epa.gov/gmpo/edresources/pleistocene.html).

U.S. Geological Survey. "The Geologic Time Scale." Retrieved September 10, 2008 (http://vulcan.wr.usgs.gov/Glossary/geo_time_scale.html).

VinceLombardi.com. "Biography." Retrieved November 17, 2008 (http://vincelombardi.com/about/bio2.htm).

Wisconsin Emergency Management. "Wisconsin's Winter Awareness Week." October 29, 2004. Retrieved September 8, 2008 (http://emergencymanagement.wi.gov/docview.asp?docid = 1132).

Wisconsin Historical Society. "James Duane Doty." Retrieved November 15, 2008 (http://www.wisconsinhistory.org/topics/doty).

Wisconsin Historical Society. "The Land Where We Stand." Retrieved September 8, 2008 (http://www.wisconsinhistory.org/teachers/lessons/pdf/learning.pdf).

Wisconsin Historical Society. "Turning Points in Wisconsin History." Retrieved September 1, 8, 13, and 24; October 8, 9, 14, 16, and 17; and November 3, 5, 6, and 17, 2008 (http://www.wisconsinhistory.org/turningpoints).

Wisconsin State Cartographer's Office. "Wisconsin Statistics." Retrieved November 10, 2008 (http://www.sco.wisc.edu/maps/WIstatistics.php).

Wisconsin State Climatology Office. "Statewide Wisconsin Climate." Retrieved November 12, 2008 (http://www.aos.wisc.edu/~sco/clim-history/state).

WisconsinStories.com. "Wisconsin Hometown Stories: Green Bay." Transcript. Wisconsin Public Television, November 12, 2007. Retrieved November 4, 2008 (http://www.wisconsinstories.org/greenbay/transcript.cfm).

WorldAtlas.com. "Wisconsin: Famous Natives." Retrieved November 1, 2008 (http://www.worldatlas.com/webimage/countrys/namerica/usstates/wifamous.htm).

INDEX

About the Author

At the start of her journalism career, Bridget Heos wrote history articles for newspapers and magazines about her hometown of Kansas City. Now, she is the author of four children's nonfiction books. She enjoys writing about states because, even though they are united, each has a unique history and culture.

Photo Credits

Cover (top left), pp. 15, 16, 20, 21, 22, 29 Wisconsin Historical Society; cover (top right), p. 24 Karen Bleier/AFP/Getty Images; cover (bottom) Scott Olson/Getty Images; pp. 3, 6, 13, 19, 25, 31, 39 © www.istockphoto.com/steverts; p. 4 (top) © GeoAtlas; p. 7 Kevin Horan/Stone/Getty Images; p. 9 © AP Images; p. 11 © Tom Bean/Corbis; pp. 14, 41 (right) Wikimedia Commons; p. 17 Library of Congress Geography and Map Division; p. 26 © Ralf-Finn Hestoft/Corbis; pp. 27, 32, 37 Library of Congress Prints and Photographs Division; p. 33 FPG/Hulton Archive/Getty Images; p. 35 © Bettmann Corbis; p. 36 Jonathan Daniel/Allsport/Getty Images; p. 40 (left) Courtesy of Robesus, Inc.; p. 41 (left) © www.istockphoto.com/Aleksander Bolbot.

Designer: Les Kanturek; Editor: Bethany Bryan;
Photo Researcher: Cindy Reiman